Special Days Poems

Compiled by John Foster

D0522494

Contents

Acknowledgements

The Editor and Publisher wish to thank the following who have kindly given permission for the use of copyright material:

John Foster for 'Pancake Day' © 1991 John Foster; Gwenda Izzet for 'My birthday' © 1991 Gwenda Izzet; Ian Larmont for 'Holi' © 1991 Ian Larmont; Wendy Larmont for 'Chinese New Year' © 1991 Wendy Larmont; Judith Nicholls for 'Christmas Eve' © 1991 Judith Nicholls; Marian Swinger for 'Eid-Mubarak' © 1991 Marian Swinger; Irene Yates for 'At Bimla's house last night' © 1991 Irene Yates.

My birthday

My birthday's on Monday.
I'll be six years old.
I'll have a big cake
With letters of gold.
The letters will say
'Happy birthday to you!'
My friends will all eat it
And teacher will too.

Gwenda Izzet

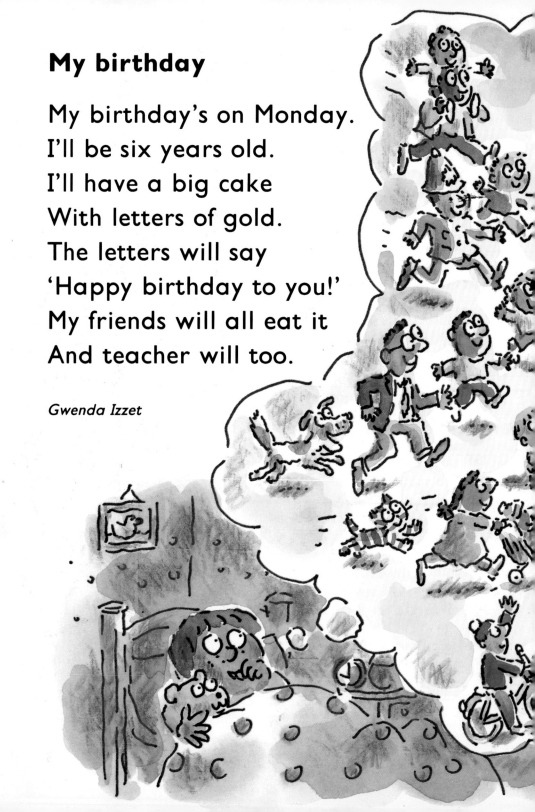

Bonfire Night

In the night-time darkness,
In the night-time cold,
Did you spot a catherine wheel
Raining showers of gold?
Did you watch a rocket
Go zoom into the sky?
And hear a bonfire crackle
As the sparks lit up the guy?
In the night-time darkness,
In the night-time cold,
Did you clutch a sparkler
As it scattered stars of gold?

Irene Yates

5

Pancake Day

It's Pancake Day!
It's Pancake Day!
Hurry home to tea!
There'll be pancakes for you!
There'll be pancakes for me!

Dad's cooking pancakes
In the frying pan,
Turning them by tossing them
As high as he can.

It's Pancake Day!
It's Pancake Day!
Sit down for your tea.
There are pancakes for you!
There are pancakes for me!

Dad's made some pancakes,
Crisp and golden brown,
Sprinkle them with sugar
And gobble them down!

John Foster

Eid-Mubarak

There's Granny, Uncle, Aunty,
my cousins at the back.
They're hugging Mum and Daddy.
We cry, 'Eid-Mubarak.'
We've had lots of cards
and presents,
there's a knocking at the door.
Can it be my Grandad
bringing us some more?
Yes, it's really Grandad.
What's that behind his back?
We hug him in the hallway
and shout, 'Eid-Mubarak.'

Marian Swinger

8

At Bimla's house last night

At Bimla's house last night
We had fireworks and
Sparklers and rice and
Sweet, juicy
Jum-jums bigger than
Gobstoppers.

At Bimla's house last night
Her Dad lit up
All the rooms with candles
And down in the kitchen
Her Mum was so pleased
She gave me a hug.
At Bimla's house last night
We all sang
Songs and wished each other

Happy Divali!

Irene Yates

11

Christmas Eve

Nearly midnight;
still can't sleep!
Has he been yet?
Dare I peep?

Sneak out softly,
creaking floor!
Down the stairs
and through the door . . .
In the darkness
by the tree,
tightly wrapped . . .
but which for me?

Feel the ribbon,
find the card!
This one? That one?
Heart thumps hard.
Trembling fingers,
throbbing head,
then . . .

a voice yells

'BACK TO BED!'

Judith Nicholls

Chinese New Year

Dragons, lions,
Red and gold.
In with the New Year,
Out with the old.

Banners flying,
Bands playing.
Lion prancing,
Dragon swaying.

Fireworks cracking,
Lanterns swinging,
People laughing,
Dancing, singing.

Dragons, lions,
Red and gold.
In with the New Year,
Out with the Old.

Wendy Larmont

15

Holi

How are you?
Ready to throw?
Get the paint,
Off we go!

Ian Larmont